Health
and Wellness

Prevention | Getting Medical Attention
Handling Health Problems | Dealing With Stress

LIFE SKILLS

HANDBOOKS

Car and Driver
Community Resources and Safety
Consumer Spending
Everyday Household Tasks
Getting Ahead at Work
Health and Wellness
Managing Money
Moving Out on Your Own
Transportation
Workplace Readiness

Copyright © 2022 by Saddleback Educational Publishing

All rights reserved. No part of this book may be reproduced in any form or by any means, electronic or mechanical, including photocopying, recording, scanning, or by any information storage and retrieval system, without the written permission of the publisher. SADDLEBACK EDUCATIONAL PUBLISHING and any associated logos are trademarks and/or registered trademarks of Saddleback Educational Publishing.

ISBN: 978-1-68021-986-9
eBook: 978-1-64598-784-0

Printed in Malaysia
26 25 24 23 22   1 2 3 4 5

TABLE OF CONTENTS

Section 1: Prevention 5
- Chapter 1: Physical Fitness 8
- Chapter 2: Nutrition 16
- Chapter 3: Hygiene 20
- Chapter 4: Stopping the Spread of Infectious Diseases 28

Section 2: Getting Medical Attention 33
- Chapter 1: Health Insurance 36
- Chapter 2: The Doctor's Office 42
- Chapter 3: Dental Treatment 49
- Chapter 4: Surgery 56

Section 3: Handling Health Problems 63
- Chapter 1: Recognizing Warning Signs 66
- Chapter 2: First Aid and Emergency Care 72
- Chapter 3: Prescription and Over-the-Counter Medicines 77
- Chapter 4: Mental Health 87

Section 4: Dealing With Stress 95
- Chapter 1: The Effects of Stress on the Body 98
- Chapter 2: Recognizing Stressors 103
- Chapter 3: Finding Ways to Cope 106
- Chapter 4: Post-Traumatic Stress Disorder 110

Glossary 116

SECTION 1

Prevention

Many people take their good health for granted. Then something happens. A bone might break. Illness strikes. Visits to the doctor become more frequent. Developing healthy habits is vital to protecting your health. Regular exercise, good hygiene, proper nutrition, and accident prevention can go a long way toward keeping you feeling good.

Making Good Health a Habit

Hector hated missing school, but he was sick. Thankfully, he wouldn't have to be out too long. His doctor said it was just a mild case of the flu.

Last weekend, Hector had gone to his friend Scott's house. That must have been when he caught the illness. Scott had invited a few friends over to watch movies. One girl had the sniffles and a cough. She left early and was out of school the next day.

Hector usually did everything he could to avoid getting sick. Living in a house with five other people made that a challenge. His mother reminded everyone to wash their hands to prevent the spread of germs. She teased Hector about "not having time to get sick."

Normally, Hector got a flu shot every year. But this year he did not. He had been too busy with his job, school, and working out. The shot hadn't been a priority. Now Hector wished he'd made time for it.

Chapter 1
Physical Fitness

Think about the challenges your body faces each day. Do you run to the bus stop? Is your backpack heavy and hard to carry? After school, do you play a sport?

Your body's ability to meet these daily demands is called physical fitness. Regular exercise is one of the keys to physical fitness. It is part of a healthy lifestyle and helps you look and feel your best.

Aerobic Exercise

Getting regular exercise can help you live a longer and healthier life. Aerobic exercise strengthens your heart. During aerobic exercise, you breathe in more oxygen, and your body uses it in an effective way. This type of exercise makes your heart beat faster. More blood is pumped to your muscles, which gives them more oxygen. Swimming, biking, walking, and running are examples of aerobic exercise.

How much aerobic exercise is enough? The Mayo Clinic says to do at least 30 minutes of aerobic activity a day.

Walking as Aerobic Exercise

- **Leisure walking:** Stroll at a slow to moderate pace.

- **Race walking or power walking:** This form of walking comes close to running, but unlike running, at least one foot remains on the ground at all times. To do it, pick up your pace and pump your arms.

- **Hill walking:** After walking on flat ground at a moderate pace for five to ten minutes, walk up a hill at a steady pace. Then walk down the hill and back up again.

- **Interval training:** Start with a warm-up by walking at a slow pace for five to ten minutes. Next, walk as quickly as you can for 20 seconds. Then walk at a normal pace for 40 to 60 seconds. Continue to switch back and forth between a fast pace and a normal speed.

Balance

Balance isn't often something we think about when it comes to health. However, improving balance is an important part of staying healthy. Good balance makes you feel steadier on your feet and helps prevent falls. Posture is an important part of balance. This is the way your body is positioned when sitting or standing. When the body is positioned well, you are less likely to fall or injure yourself. To maintain good balance and posture, strong muscles are key.

Strength Training

Having big muscles doesn't necessarily mean that a person is healthy. But being strong is an important aspect of good health. It gives you the ability to lift objects without injury.

Strengthening your muscles doesn't just make you stronger. It also stimulates bone growth, lowers blood sugar, helps with weight control, improves balance and posture, and reduces stress and pain in the lower back.

Lifting weights is one way to improve strength. If you don't have dumbbells or can't get to the gym, don't worry. Bodyweight exercises like squats, push-ups, and lunges are effective ways to build muscle without equipment.

Play It Safe

Exercise is a must for good health, but be sure to work out safely.

Warm up first to loosen your muscles before you put them to work. Stretch before and after exercising to reduce the chance of injury.

After your activity, make sure to give your muscles time to cool down and relax.

Guidelines for Stretching

- Don't stretch your muscles when they're cold. Walk at a slow pace for five or ten minutes before doing your warm-up stretches.
- After exercising, stretch again.
- Stretch all of your major muscle groups, not just your legs.
- Be sure to stretch both sides of your body.
- Don't bounce when you stretch. Instead, hold the stretch for approximately 30 seconds. Repeat each stretch three or four times.
- Avoid stretching to the point that it hurts. You should feel tension, not pain.
- Add movement to your stretching. For instance, reach up or out with your arms while stretching your legs. Think of the movements used in yoga and martial arts.

Benefits of Exercise

Many people who exercise regularly say they love it. Why? Scientists have found that the body releases special chemicals during exercise. These are called *endorphins*. They create a sense of well-being. Endorphins also reduce feelings of stress.

Exercise has other benefits too. These include:

- helping you maintain a healthy weight
- improving mental function
- reducing your risk of heart disease
- helping the body manage blood sugar levels
- improving sleep
- reducing the risk for certain cancers

How to Incorporate Exercise Into Your Life

Finding time to squeeze in a workout can be hard. These tips will help you weave exercise into your daily life.

- Take the stairs instead of the elevator.
- Go for a walk on your lunch break.
- Work out when you wake up. Before getting dressed for the day, do a few push-ups or crunches.
- Wear a pedometer to see how many steps you can get in during the day. A good target for healthy adults is 10,000 steps.
- Dance or do other movements while doing housework.

Chapter 2
Nutrition

Eating nutritious foods is another important step you can take to keep yourself healthy. A nutritious diet gives you energy and helps you stay fit.

Good Nutrition Basics

To maintain proper nutrition, your body must get all the **nutrients**, **vitamins**, and **minerals** it needs in order to function at its best. But what does that look like in practice? The following tips can help you plan meals geared toward better nutrition.

1. **Eat whole grains.** Whole grains include oats, brown rice, bulgur, barley, and rye. These are high in fiber, B vitamins, and protein. They help lower your risk of heart disease, stroke, and diabetes.

2. **Vary your veggies.** Choose a mix of colors of vegetables: green, red, orange, and yellow. Different-colored vegetables have different health benefits.

3. **Focus on fruits.** Eat fresh fruit, rather than canned or frozen, as much as possible. Drink 100% fruit juice. Flavored fruit drinks often contain a lot of sugar and little actual juice.

4. **Eat calcium-rich foods.** Calcium is important for building strong bones.

5. **Go lean with protein.** Meat is a good source of protein. But look for lean cuts of meat. Beans and nuts are also good sources of protein.

There are many types of diets out there that claim to offer a variety of health benefits. You may have a condition that restricts your diet too. It can be hard to know how to maintain proper nutrition. Talk to your doctor about how you can eat better for your body.

Understanding Nutrition Facts Labels

Most packaged foods sold in the grocery store have a nutrition facts label. This is meant to give consumers important information about the food. However, these labels are not always easy to understand. The following is an example of a nutrition facts label with some helpful tips on how to read it.

Sample Nutrition Facts Label for Boxed Mac and Cheese

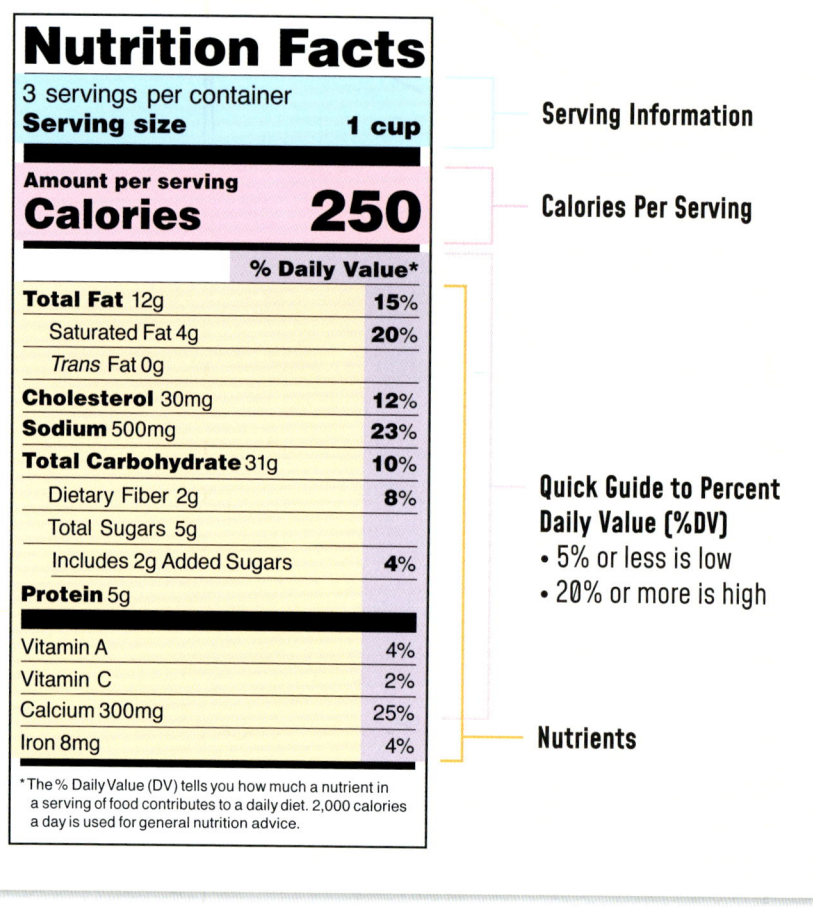

Know What You're Eating

The U.S. Food and Drug Administration (FDA) requires that food companies live up to the claims they make about their products. To be sure of what you're eating, look for these terms on product labels:

- **"Free," as in "sugar-free":** The product contains none or almost none of the ingredient.

- **"Fresh," as in "fresh grapefruit":** The product is raw and has not been heated or frozen.

- **"High," as in "high in fiber":** The product provides 20% or more of the daily value (DV) of the nutrient per serving.

- **"Light" or "Lite," as in "lite cream cheese":** The product's label must say how it's different from the original version of the food. For example, it may contain one-third fewer calories or one-half the fat or sodium of the regular product.

- **"A good source," as in "a good source of calcium":** A serving of the product provides 10 to 19% of the DV of the nutrient named.

Chapter 3
Hygiene

Did you know that bathing helps you maintain good health too? People look and feel better when they're clean. Good hygiene habits also help protect you from germs that can lead to anything from minor colds to major life-threatening illnesses.

Improving Your Hygiene

Are you doing enough to keep yourself clean and healthy? Follow these steps to improve your hygiene and health.

Guarding Against Germs

- Shower or bathe regularly.

- Wash your hands often with soap and water for at least 20 seconds. This is about how long it takes to sing the "Happy Birthday" song twice. Make sure to wash the fronts and backs of your hands and between all of your fingers.

- Dry your hands with a clean towel after washing.

- When sneezing, cover your nose with a tissue. If you don't have one, sneeze into your upper sleeve.

- When you cough, cover your mouth with a tissue, the back of your hand, or the crook of your elbow.

Using Hand Sanitizers

Washing your hands is a good way to stay healthy. Soap and water are best for getting rid of germs. Hand sanitizers can also help prevent their spread. Here are the benefits and drawbacks of using hand sanitizers:

Benefits

- Hand sanitizers with at least 60% alcohol can kill most bacteria (germs).
- They may come in small bottles that are easy to carry with you.
- People can use them when soap and water aren't available.

Drawbacks

- Hand sanitizers don't kill or remove all germs.
- They won't wash away dirt. You need soap and water for that.
- Both good and bad bacteria can be killed. Good bacteria help you stay healthy.
- Because of their alcohol content, hand sanitizers are flammable.
- The contents are poisonous if swallowed.

Avoiding Germs in Public Restrooms

- Don't set your belongings on the counter or floor.
- Use a piece of toilet paper when flushing the toilet to avoid touching the handle.
- Wash your hands thoroughly with soap and water.
- Use your forearm or elbow to push the button or lever to get a paper towel.
- Use a clean paper towel to turn off the faucet after you've washed your hands.
- Try not to touch the surface of a hot-air hand dryer.
- When you're ready to leave, use a paper towel to open the door.

Caring for Your Hair and Scalp

- Wash your hair regularly.

- Follow the directions on the shampoo bottle.

- Regularly clean your combs, brushes, and pillowcases.

- Never share hats, combs, or brushes.

What's Wrong With Sharing?

Sharing items such as combs, brushes, hats, and pillows can cause health problems like head lice. These are tiny insects that nest and lay eggs in the hair. Lice make the scalp itch, and scratching can lead to sores and infection. In rare cases, lice can even cause hair to fall out.

Getting rid of lice can be hard. You need to wash your hair with special shampoo that contains a medicine. Combs, brushes, and bedding must also be washed. Clothing such as hats and scarves may need to be thrown away.

To prevent lice, don't share items that touch the hair. Avoid close contact with someone who has lice.

Taking Care of Your Teeth

- Brush your teeth every morning and night and after eating.
- Brush both the outside and inside surfaces of your teeth.
- Brush your tongue to remove germs that can cause bad breath.
- Rinse your mouth well with water or mouthwash after brushing.
- Floss your teeth at least once a day.
- Have regular dental checkups.
- Eat a well-balanced diet.
- Avoid sugary foods and drinks.

Taking Care of Your Skin

- Drink plenty of water. Aim for at least eight glasses a day.
- Wash your face at least twice a day. In the morning and before bed are good times.
- Also wash your face after workouts or sweating.
- Learn your skin type (dry, oily, or combination) and use skin care products that are right for you.
- Keep your hair clean and off your face.
- Avoid squeezing pimples and blackheads.
- See a *dermatologist* about *severe* skin problems.

Acne

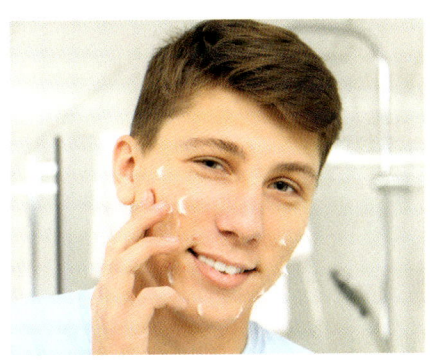

Acne is a skin condition that usually appears on the face, shoulders, and back. It's commonly called pimples or zits. Acne occurs when your pores—the tiny holes on the surface of your skin—become clogged with oil, dirt, and bacteria. This causes whiteheads, blackheads, and swollen, red bumps to form. The bumps are sometimes called blemishes.

How can you treat acne?

1. **Start with self-care.**
   - Wash your skin once or twice a day (including after exercise) with mild soap.
   - If your hair is oily, shampoo it every day.
   - Keep your hair away from your face.
   - Stay away from sugary and starchy foods, such as white bread, white rice, pasta, and potatoes.
   - Don't squeeze, scratch, pick, or rub pimples.
   - Avoid touching your face.
   - If you wear makeup, avoid oily products. Remove all makeup at night.
   - Don't wear headbands or hats that touch your forehead or the sides of your face.
2. **Next, try the drugstore.** Ask the pharmacist to suggest an over-the-counter acne medicine.
3. **Finally, see your doctor.** If you're still having acne problems, see your doctor and ask about a prescription medicine.

Chapter 4
Stopping the Spread of Infectious Diseases

Most of us spend our days with other people. That means we live among germs. These can be **viruses** or **bacteria**. Most germs aren't harmful, but some are **infectious**.

Because germs spread from person to person, we're all likely to catch an illness now and then. Mostly, we come down with short-term **ailments**, like a cold or the flu. But some infectious diseases are serious health threats.

Social Activities With Health Risks

To stay healthy, you need to understand infectious diseases and make efforts not to contract them. The following sections describe some social activities that may put you at risk for infection. You can stay safe by avoiding high-risk activities and by protecting yourself when you do participate in them.

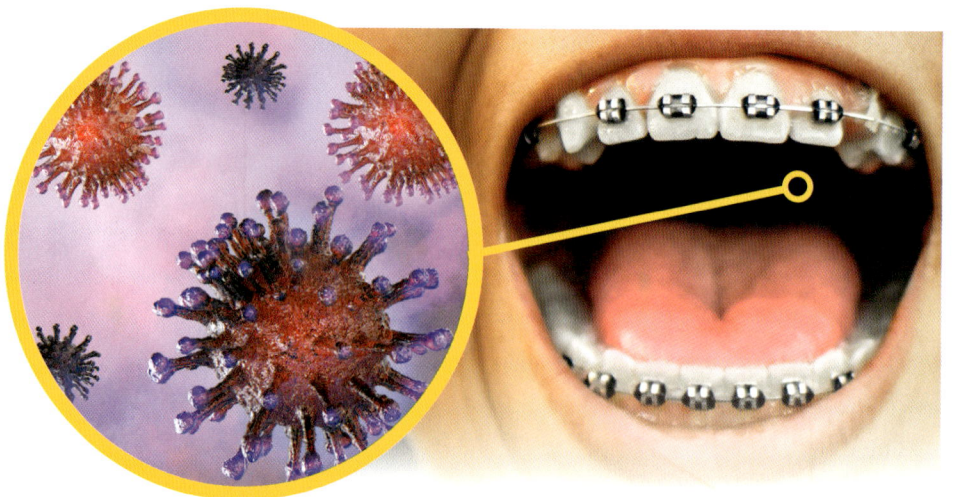

Day-to-Day Contact

- **Infectious mononucleosis used to be called "the kissing disease."** That's because it's common among teens and young adults. Mono, as this virus is called, is usually spread by contact with an infected person's saliva. Early symptoms of mono are lack of energy, a feeling of tiredness, a lack of appetite, and chills. Sore throat, fever, and swollen glands develop within a few days. To prevent the spread of mono, avoid kissing or sharing drinks, food, or other personal items with people who have it.

- **Strep throat is a sore throat caused by streptococcal bacteria.** Symptoms include fever and swollen glands in the neck. School-aged children and teenagers get strep most often. However, it's very contagious and spreads easily among members of the same household. Strep is spread by contact with saliva and droplets from sneezing and coughing. To prevent the spread of strep, cover your mouth and nose when you sneeze. Also wash your hands often with soap and water for at least 20 seconds.

Piercing and Tattooing

- **Skin infections are a risk when getting a piercing or tattoo.** Symptoms include redness, swelling, pain, and drainage of pus. Treatment usually requires use of an antibiotic. To avoid skin infections, make sure to only go to reputable businesses for piercings or tattoos. Ask about their sterilization practices. Carefully follow the steps to clean and care for your new piercing or tattoo.

- **Blood-borne diseases can be passed through needles used for piercings and tattoos as well.** These include hepatitis B (HBV), hepatitis C (HCV), and human immunodeficiency virus (HIV). To avoid these illnesses, never use needles that have been used by others.

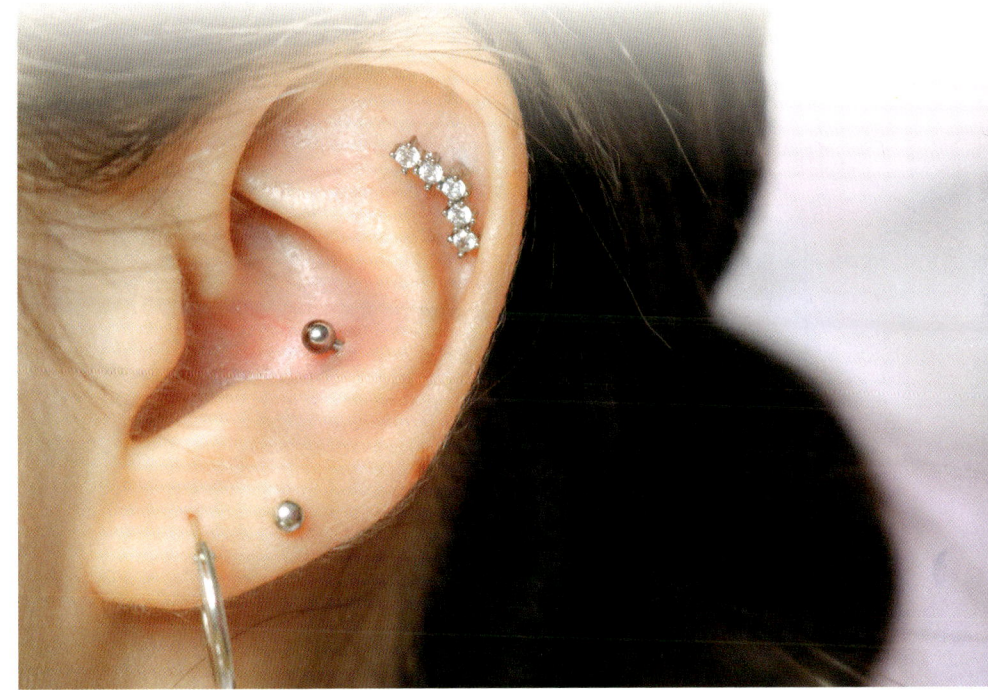

SECTION 2

Getting Medical Attention

Being unhealthy isn't just frustrating. It's also expensive. That's why it's important to have **health insurance**. Knowing that your doctors' visits will be paid for makes it more likely that you'll get medical care on a regular basis. Your regular medical care should also include visits to the dentist. If you're struggling with an emotional problem, get help from a mental health professional too.

Getting the Help You Need

Audrey was having a tough time. Six months ago, she'd lost her full-time job. The company she'd worked for laid off 20 employees.

Since then, Audrey had held two part-time jobs. Her rent and other expenses were covered. But she'd had to cut back on going out with her friends. She stayed home a lot. This got lonely.

Audrey didn't want to complain. She knew many other people were worse off than she was. But she felt like everything was going wrong.

Three weeks after losing her job, Audrey had been in a car accident. It wasn't serious. Her car had gotten only a small dent, and she didn't think she was hurt. But soon, her neck and back started to ache.

Audrey thought about going to the doctor. But because she'd lost her job, she no longer had health insurance. Getting medical attention would be expensive. She couldn't afford to pay more bills, so she didn't go.

A month or so after the accident, Audrey chipped a tooth. She wanted to go to the dentist, but she didn't have dental insurance anymore either. The tooth didn't hurt much, but she hated how it looked and felt. She decided she'd just have to live with it.

Several weeks later, Audrey and her boyfriend broke up. Things between them had been tense since Audrey's job loss. "You're so moody!" he finally told her. She had to admit that she wasn't much fun to be around.

Audrey's mother told her that things would get better. "You're just feeling blue," she said. But Audrey wasn't so sure. Her situation seemed pretty hopeless.

Chapter 1
Health Insurance

Health insurance helps people afford medical treatment. It pays for certain health-care costs, such as doctor visits, hospital stays, surgeries, and laboratory tests. Some health insurance pays for prescription medicines and devices such as glasses and hearing aids.

Types of Health Insurance Plans

Whether you're buying health insurance on your own or signing up through your employer, you have choices. Here are the main types of plans and how they differ.

- **Health maintenance organizations (HMOs):** An HMO delivers all services through a network of health-care providers. These plans often offer less freedom of choice when it comes to selecting a doctor.

- **Preferred provider organizations (PPOs):** A PPO gives you more freedom to choose your health-care provider, but there are often higher out-of-pocket costs for out-of-network doctors.

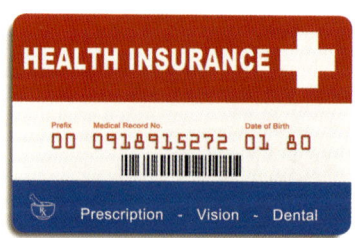

- **Exclusive provider organizations (EPOs):** EPOs offer more choices than HMOs, but provide no coverage for seeing an out-of-network provider.

- **Point-of-service (POS):** A POS plan blends features of an HMO with a PPO, offering more freedom to choose your health-care providers than you have in an HMO. POS plans also require you to choose a primary care doctor who will coordinate your care and refer you to specialists.

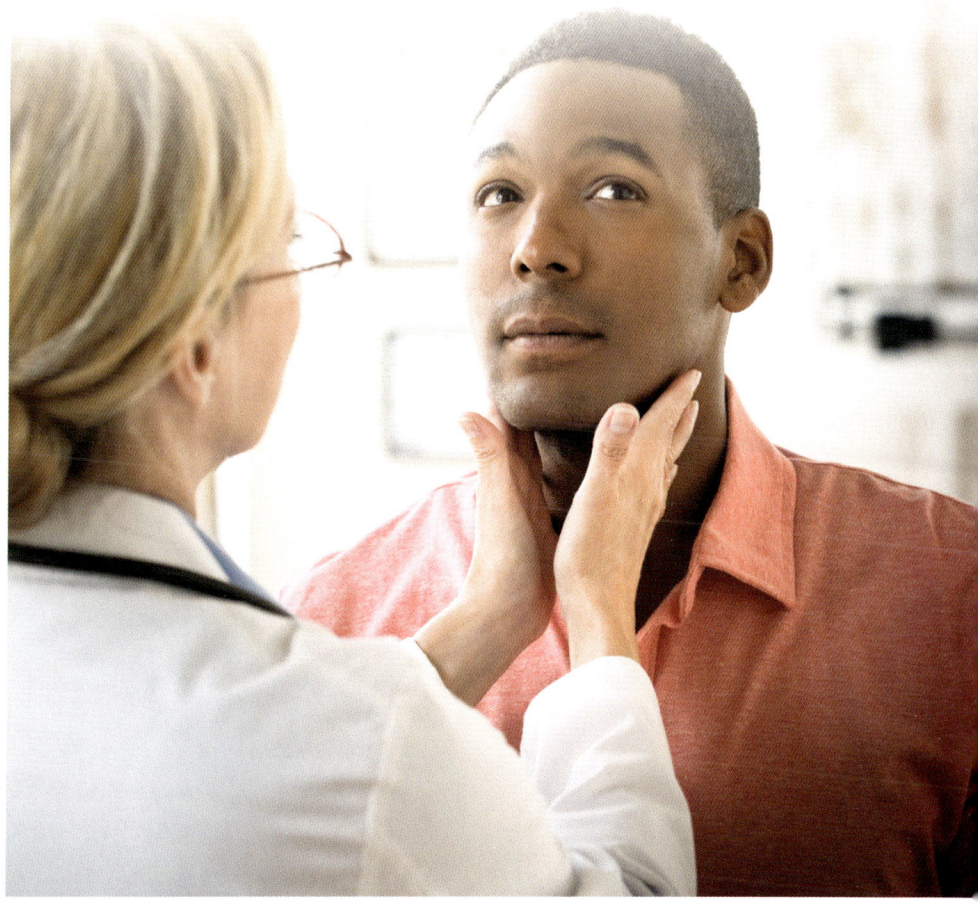

Do You Need Health Insurance?

Many young people don't think they need health insurance. They consider themselves healthy and not in need of medical care. But anyone can get sick or have an accident. Everyone should also get regular checkups.

Most people can't afford the high costs of health care without health insurance. Study the chart on the next page. It lists the average costs of three common medical treatments in the U.S. Keep in mind that there are many additional costs not listed here. These may include X-rays, lab tests, and medications. The price of a hospital stay isn't included either. Ask yourself, "Could I pay for treatment out of my pocket?" If the answer is no, then you need health insurance.

Costs of Medical Procedures Without Insurance

Medical Treatment	Sample Cost of Treatment
Liver transplant	$101,240
Gallbladder surgery	$54,041
Kidney transplant	$46,760

Some surgeries are exploratory. This means doctors aren't even sure what the medical problem is yet. They decide to do surgery to get a better look inside the body. Without insurance, exploratory chest surgery costs, on average, $137,533. Additional surgeries may be needed once doctors understand the problem. These costs can really add up.

Where Do You Get Health Insurance?

Most people get health insurance through their job. Employers offer certain kinds of coverage. Many pay part or all of the premium. Having health insurance is an important employment benefit.

If you can't get health insurance through your work, you may need to buy an individual plan. Search online to learn how to find a plan that meets your needs.

Health Coverage Through Your Parents

Are you under age 26? If so, you can remain on a parent's *policy*. In 2010, the U.S. government set this rule as part of the Affordable Care Act. You can be on a parent's plan whether or not you are any of the following:

- in school
- living with your parents
- financially *dependent* on your parents
- married

If you need to be added back onto your parent's policy, don't worry. Insurance companies offer a 30-day period each year when new people can be added.

Chapter 2
The Doctor's Office

For the last five days, Sarah has had an earache. She knows that when a health problem won't go away, it's time to call the doctor.

Sarah calls Dr. Miller's office just after it opens for the day. She talks to a nurse and explains that she's ill and would like to see the doctor. The nurse makes some notes about what Sarah tells her. Then she gives Sarah a 3:00 p.m. appointment that day.

Sarah arrives at the office at 2:45. She uses the 15 extra minutes to update her insurance information and fill out forms.

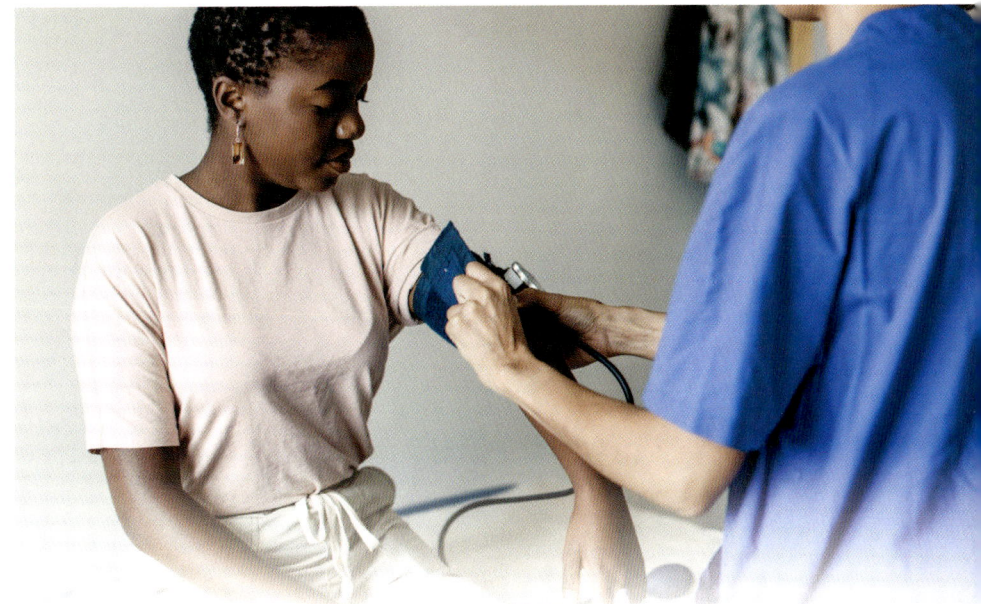

Routine Health Checks

A nurse takes Sarah to the exam room. The nurse does several routine health checks before the doctor comes in. She weighs Sarah and checks her blood pressure, pulse rate, and temperature. Then she records the information on Sarah's chart.

Why are these routine health checks important? They give doctors a view of a patient's overall health. For instance, blood pressure is the force of blood against the walls of the arteries. It tells the doctor about the strength of a patient's heart, the ease of blood flow, and the health of their arteries. High blood pressure is a serious medical condition. It can lead to other health problems.

Temperature is another important health check. The body's normal temperature is 97.5 to 98.6 degrees Fahrenheit. A temperature that's higher than normal often indicates some kind of infection.

Understanding Blood Pressure Readings

As blood pumps from your heart to the rest of your body, the pressure of the blood against your artery walls changes. Routine checks of blood pressure measure the high and low levels of pressure.

1. Systolic pressure occurs when the heart beats. The pressure is usually highest at this point.
2. Diastolic pressure occurs when the heart rests between beats. The pressure is usually lowest at this point.

Blood pressure readings, or checks, report both types of pressure. A reading is like a fraction. The systolic pressure is on the top, and the diastolic pressure is on the bottom. For a blood pressure of 110/75, you would say "110 over 75."

Both numbers are important measures of heart health. The chart below explains what they mean when combined in a blood pressure reading:

Systolic (Top) Number	Diastolic (Bottom) Number	Blood Pressure Condition	What to Do
Below 120	Below 80	Normal	Maintain or develop a healthy lifestyle.
120–129	Below 80	Elevated/ Pre-hypertension	Monitor pressure and make diet and lifestyle adjustments as needed.
130–139	80–89	Stage 1 hypertension	Develop a healthier lifestyle. Set a blood pressure goal. If you don't reach it in six months, discuss medications with your doctor.
140 or higher	90 or higher	Stage 2 hypertension (high blood pressure)	Develop a healthier lifestyle. Discuss adding blood pressure medications with your doctor.

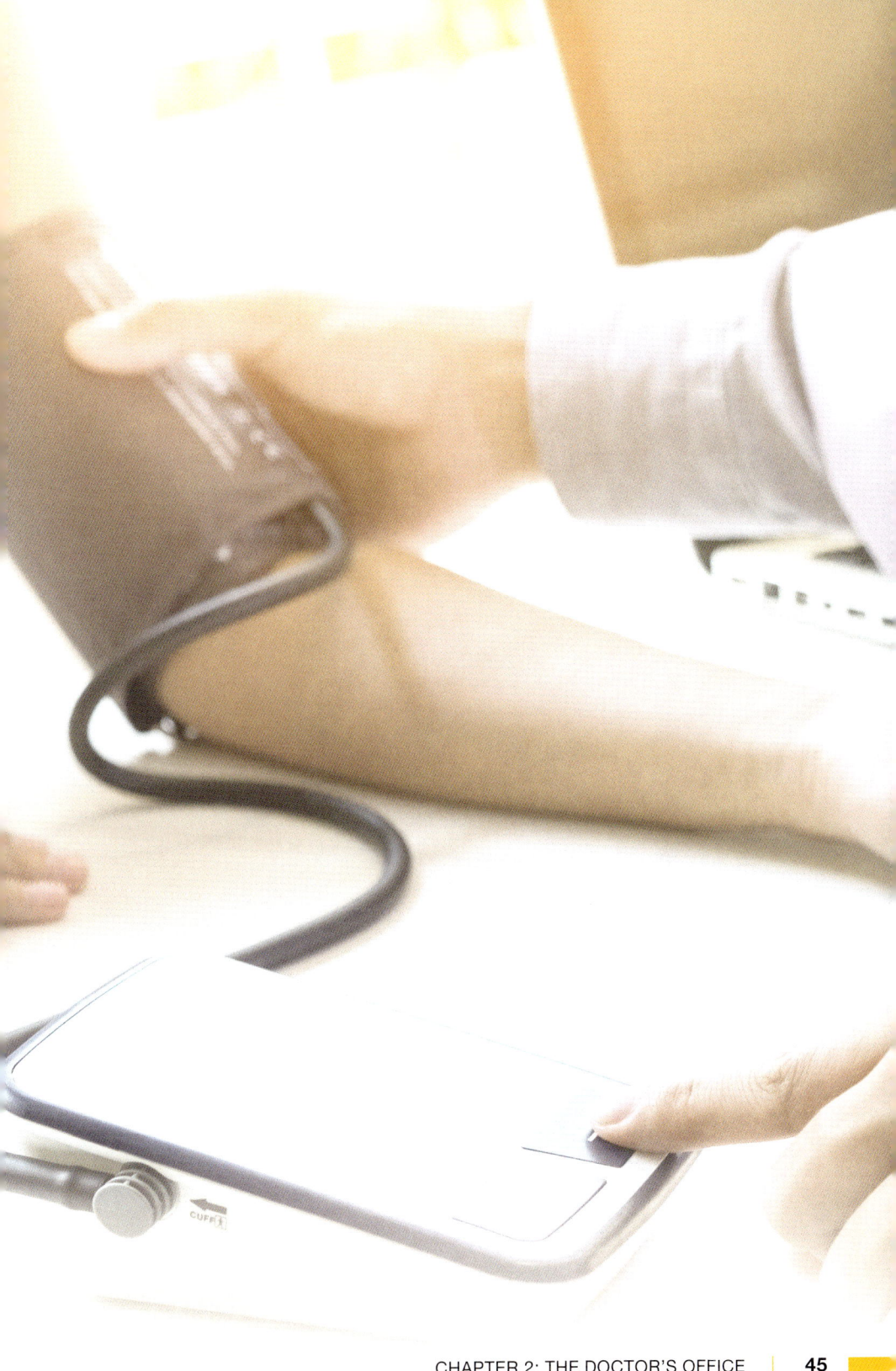

The Doctor's Examination

Alone in the exam room, Sarah checks her notes. She's come prepared to talk to the doctor.

Keeping a patient healthy isn't just the doctor's job. Patients have responsibilities too. The doctor needs information from the patient to make the right diagnosis and prescribe proper treatment. That information should include the following:

- a list of problems or concerns
- any medications or supplements currently being taken
- known allergies to medications or side effects experienced in the past
- questions to ask the doctor

Soon, Dr. Miller comes in. She is a general practitioner. That means she works with the whole body and provides regular medical care. Sometimes, if a problem is very specific or severe, Dr. Miller sends a patient to a specialist. If Sarah's ear doesn't get better, Dr. Miller will make a referral to an ear, nose, and throat specialist.

First, Dr. Miller reviews Sarah's chart. Then, she conducts a complete examination. She looks in Sarah's ear with a device called an otoscope. It lets the doctor view the ear canal and eardrum. Dr. Miller can see that Sarah has an ear infection, so she prescribes an antibiotic.

"We'll recheck your ear in ten days," Dr. Miller says. "Please make an appointment on your way out."

Medical Specialists and What They Treat

- **Allergist:** allergic reactions, such as asthma and hay fever
- **Cardiologist:** conditions that affect the heart and blood vessels
- **Dermatologist:** skin, hair, and nail conditions
- **Endocrinologist:** hormone disorders, such as diabetes, bone diseases, and problems with metabolism (the body's process of turning food into energy)
- **Geriatrician:** conditions of the elderly
- **Gynecologist:** women's reproductive system
- **Hematologist:** blood disorders
- **Obstetrician:** pregnancy and childbirth
- **Oncologist:** cancer
- **Ophthalmologist:** conditions of the eye
- **Orthopedic surgeon:** injured or diseased bones and joints
- **Pediatrician:** babies and children
- **Psychiatrist:** mental illness

Chapter 3
Dental Treatment

From chewing to smiling, your teeth get a big workout every day. You, your dentist, and the dental office staff make up the team that keeps your teeth and gums strong and healthy.

Most dental problems can be prevented with proper care. But in some cases, dental treatments are needed.

Preventive Care

The general recommendation is to have two dental checkups a year. However, your dentist may recommend more visits based on the health of your teeth. A regular visit will likely include the following:

- instructions on oral hygiene, including tooth brushing and flossing
- routine teeth cleaning
- treatments to prevent tooth decay, such as fluoride and tooth sealants
- an examination of the teeth and gums
- x-rays to check for cavities, cracks, and other problems

Common Dental Problems

Making regular visits to your dentist will help you avoid or control these problems:

- bad breath
- tooth sensitivity
- yellow teeth
- cavities
- toothaches
- gum disease
- mouth sores
- teeth grinding
- tooth erosion

Emergency Care

Most dentists will see emergency cases right away. If your own dentist isn't available, the office can usually make a referral for emergency care.

Examples of a dental emergency include:

- severe pain or bleeding of the teeth or gums
- a knocked out tooth or other tooth injury
- an infection in the mouth

Restorative Services

Dentists usually use fillings to repair the damage caused by tooth decay. Cavities can be filled with a variety of materials. These may include porcelain, silver amalgam, or gold.

Another kind of restorative service involves putting a crown over a tooth. A crown is an artificial tooth that fits over a real tooth. Crowns are sometimes called caps.

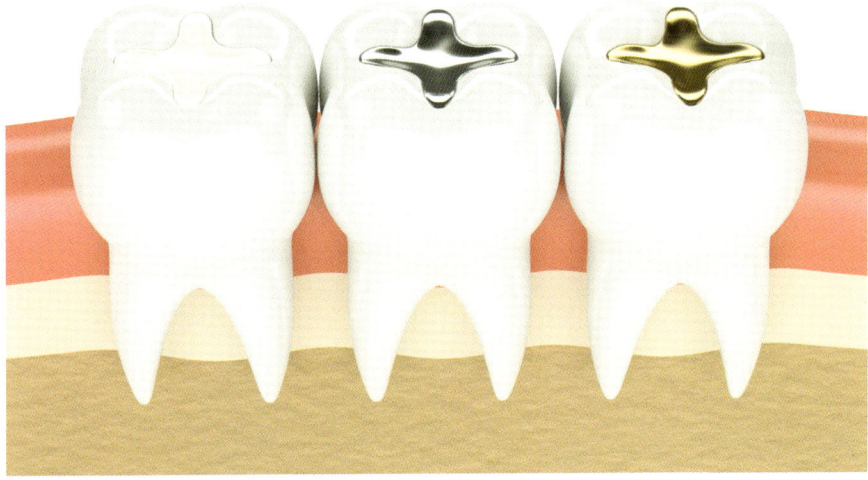

Oral Surgery

Sometimes a tooth needs to be **extracted**. This might be necessary if the tooth gets broken off or becomes **impacted**. A root canal may also be needed.

Dentists who specialize in this kind of work are called oral surgeons. Many people visit an oral surgeon to have their wisdom teeth taken out. Wisdom teeth are the last teeth people get. They usually come in during the late teens or early twenties. These teeth can cause problems, so they're often removed.

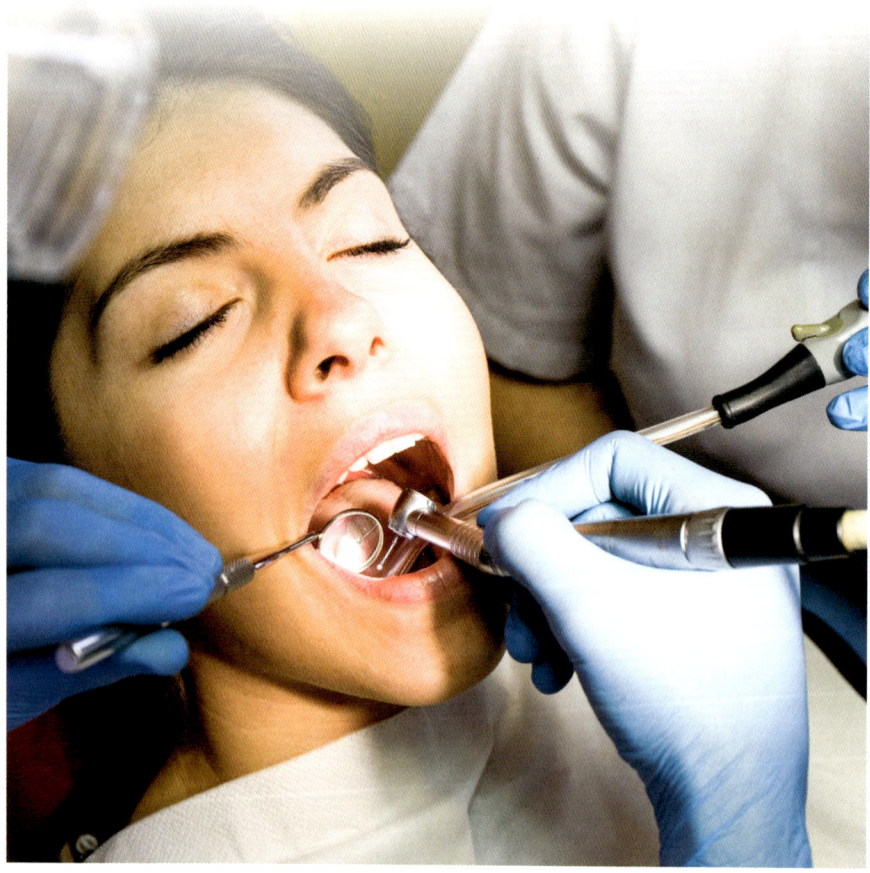

Dealing With Tooth Decay

Tooth decay is a process that gradually creates a small hole, called a cavity, in a tooth. A combination of food and bacteria causes the decay. The bacteria in your mouth feed on sugars in the food you eat. Then these germs produce acids that eat away at your teeth. When a cavity forms, your tooth may ache or feel sensitive.

How can you prevent tooth decay?

- Brush your teeth and tongue at least twice a day.
- Use toothpaste that contains fluoride.
- Floss your teeth once a day.
- Rinse daily with a mouthwash that kills bacteria.
- Limit sweet snacks and drinks.
- Eat foods containing calcium, such as dairy products.
- Visit your dentist regularly.

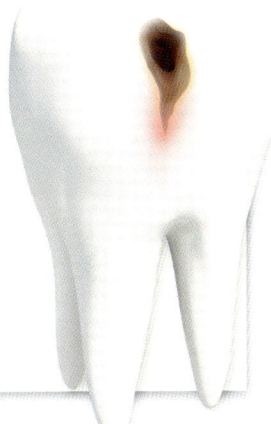

Orthodontic Services

Straight, evenly spaced teeth create a great smile. They also help a person bite and chew correctly.

An orthodontist is a dentist who specializes in straightening crooked teeth. Many children and teens visit an orthodontist to have braces put on. Adults can get braces too. Orthodontists also fit people for retainers. These help keep teeth straight once braces are removed.

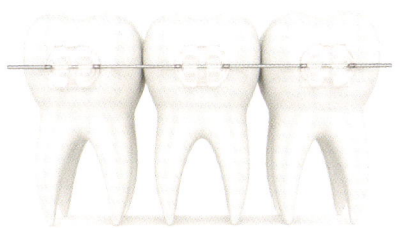

Cosmetic Treatments

Some dental treatments are done for the purpose of improving appearance. For instance, bleaching teeth, or "whitening," has become a popular cosmetic service. Dentists may also use porcelain to hide dental flaws and to improve someone's bite or smile.

Pain Control

Modern dental treatments are usually pain-free, thanks to skilled dentists and the use of local anesthetics such as lidocaine. A local anesthetic is a drug that makes a specific area numb and thus pain-free.

Dental work that's likely to be uncomfortable may be done under a general anesthetic. This puts the patient to sleep so they do not feel anything during the procedure.

Dental Insurance

Many people get dental insurance as a job benefit from their employer. Other people buy their own insurance because of the high cost of dental care. Having dental insurance helps control what you have to pay for dental work. Like health insurance, dental insurance can prevent you from going into debt if you have serious problems.

Basic dental insurance covers these kinds of dental work:

- **Preventive care and diagnostics (testing):** Most policies cover two visits a year for a checkup or exam, cleaning, X-rays, and treatments that prevent decay and gum disease.
- **Basic restorative care:** Many policies cover half or more of the cost of fillings, crowns, extractions, repairing chipped teeth, and sometimes doing root canals.
- **Major dental work:** Some plans cover at least part of the cost of work such as oral surgery and braces.

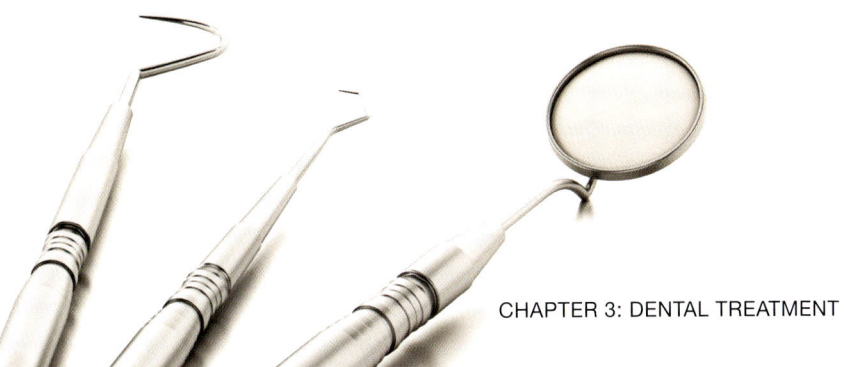

Chapter 4
Surgery

Sometimes a medical issue cannot be fixed with medication or lifestyle changes alone. For example, your appendix may be inflamed, or you might have a severely broken bone. Then your doctor may recommend surgery.

Preparing for Surgery

While the idea of surgery can be scary, being prepared can take some of that fear away. The following are steps you should take to prepare for an upcoming surgery.

- **Talk to your surgeon about what to expect from the procedure.** Also discuss risks, healing time, and any other questions you might have.

- **Ask about anesthesia.** Will you only need a local anesthetic, or will you need to be asleep during the surgery?

- **Discuss how you should physically prepare.** This usually includes not eating or drinking the night before surgery. You may need to take a special medication beforehand too.

- **Talk about what happens next.** Will you need to stay in the hospital after surgery? How much pain can be expected? Is physical therapy needed during recovery? When can you return to work?

- **Prepare your home.** If your recovery will involve being off your feet or in physical therapy, think about how to best prepare your home. Will you need assistance for daily living? What special equipment will be required? If your home has stairs, will you be able to get up and down them?

- **Try to relax.** Once you have discussed the surgery plan and all your concerns with your surgeon, try to relax. Yoga or meditation can help relieve stress and allow you to mentally prepare for surgery.

Questions to Ask Before and After Surgery

Before

- Why is this procedure needed?
- Are there any nonsurgical alternatives to this procedure?
- What are the possible risks or complications from having this surgery?
- What is the surgeon's experience with this type of surgery?
- Where will the surgery be performed?
- What type of anesthesia will be given?
- What will this surgery cost?

After

- Were there any complications during surgery?
- How long will recovery take?
- Will I need follow-up appointments?
- Can I expect any side effects?
- Will I need any medications or post-operative care?
- Will I need physical therapy?
- Do I need a nurse or special equipment at home while I recover?

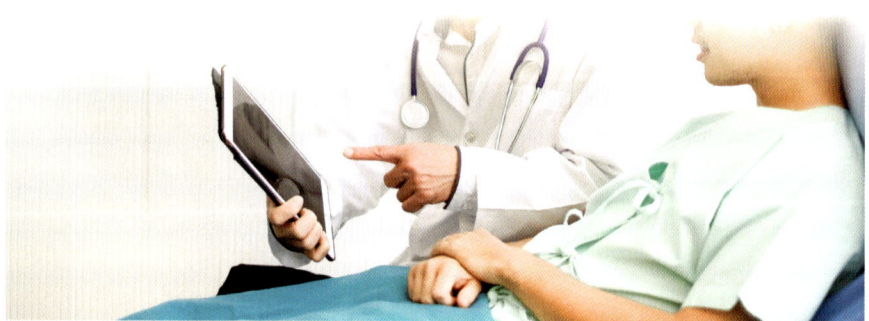

Recovery at Home

The recovery phase following surgery is very important. A smooth transition from hospital to home will help speed up your recovery.

Depending on the type of surgery you have, you may need to make some adjustments at home. If you won't be able to climb stairs, make sure you have a place to sleep, bathe, and eat on the main level of your home.

Make sure to stock up on food before surgery, especially if you will need to be on a special diet. Practice safety measures in your home as well. Use a walker or crutches if you need them. Wear flat shoes or slippers. Remove clutter and any slippery rugs. This will prevent falls. If you experience any new symptoms, such as fever or worsening pain, see your doctor right away.

Common Surgical Procedures

- **Appendectomy:** removal of the appendix to treat acute appendicitis
- **Carotid endarterectomy:** removal of a blockage from carotid arteries in the neck that supply blood to the brain
- **Cataract surgery:** removal of a lens in the eye that has been clouded by cataracts, which is replaced with a clear artificial lens implant
- **Cesarean section (C-section):** the surgical delivery of a baby by an incision through the mother's abdomen and uterus
- **Cholecystectomy:** removal of the gallbladder (a pear-shaped sac near the right lobe of the liver that holds bile)
- **Debridement of a wound, burn, or infection:** removal of foreign material and/or dead, damaged, or infected tissue from a wound or burn
- **Tonsillectomy:** removal of one or both tonsils

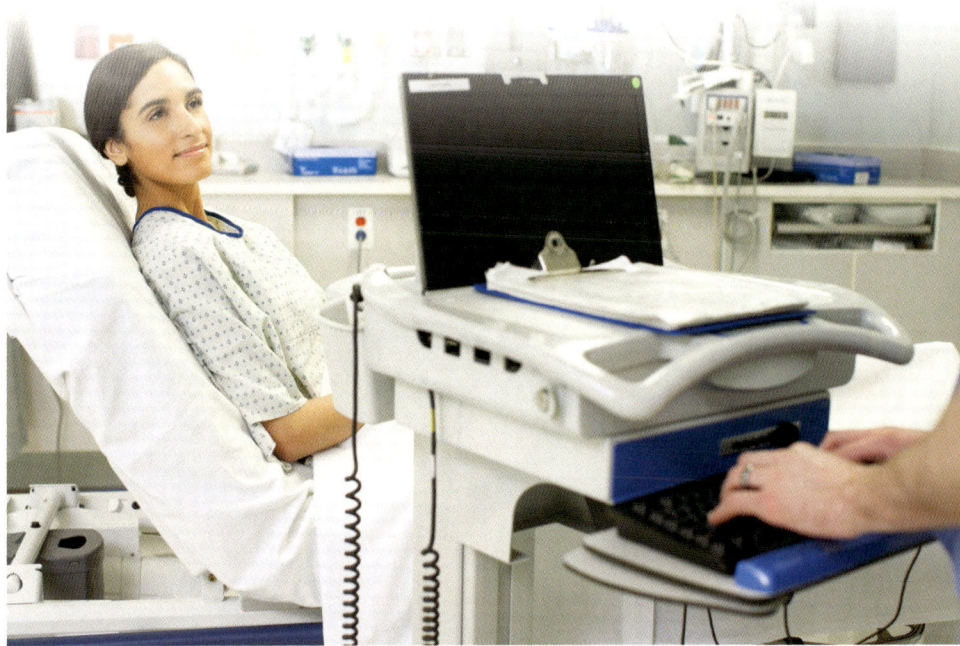

SECTION 3

Handling Health Problems

How sick do you have to be before you go see a doctor? Knowing common signs of illness can help you make that decision. It can also help you know what kind of medicine you may need to get better. Perhaps most important of all, knowing common signs of illness can help you decide when the situation is an emergency.

Playing Doctor

Ronda hadn't felt good for several days. She was achy and sweaty. Her throat was scratchy too.

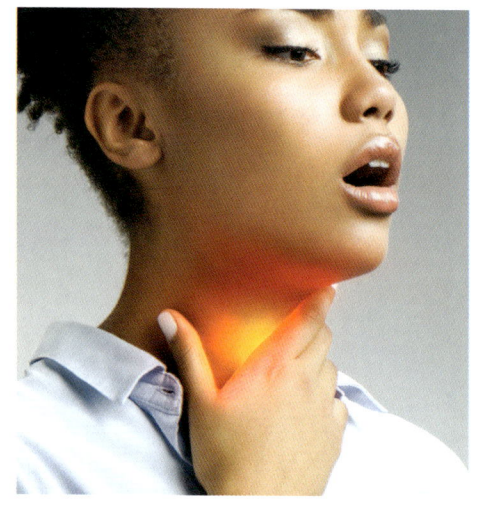

"I probably have the flu," she thought. She'd read online about the start of flu season. Ronda looked through the medicine cabinet in her family's home. There was probably something there that would help her feel better. Should she take a pain reliever? Would throat lozenges help?

Ronda decided to take cold and flu medicine. The signs of illness listed on the package matched her own symptoms pretty closely. She read the directions carefully. They said to drink a small cup of the medicine twice a day. That's what she did.

The next day, Ronda felt even worse. Her throat was so sore she could barely swallow, and she felt achier and hotter. She wished she had a thermometer to take her temperature. Ronda was sure she had a fever.

Ronda called in sick to work. She told her supervisor, Karen, what was wrong. Karen insisted that Ronda go to the doctor.

After speaking with Karen, Ronda called her doctor's office. She told the nurse how she felt.

"Come in right away," the nurse told her. "We're seeing a lot of strep throat right now."

At the doctor's office, the nurse took Ronda's temperature. She had a fever of 102 degrees. Then the doctor ran a couple of tests. Soon, the results were clear. Ronda had strep throat.

The doctor gave Ronda a prescription for an antibiotic, which is a bacteria-killing medicine. That's what she needed to get well. Ronda wished she had gone to the doctor sooner.

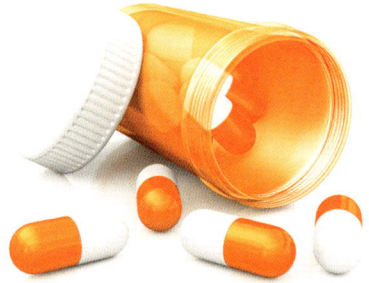

Chapter 1
Recognizing Warning Signs

When your car's warning light comes on, it tells you something is wrong. In a similar way, your body uses warning signs such as pain and fever to signal trouble.

It's important to pay attention to what your body tells you. To do that, you need to become familiar with the symptoms of common health problems. If you notice these symptoms, get help.

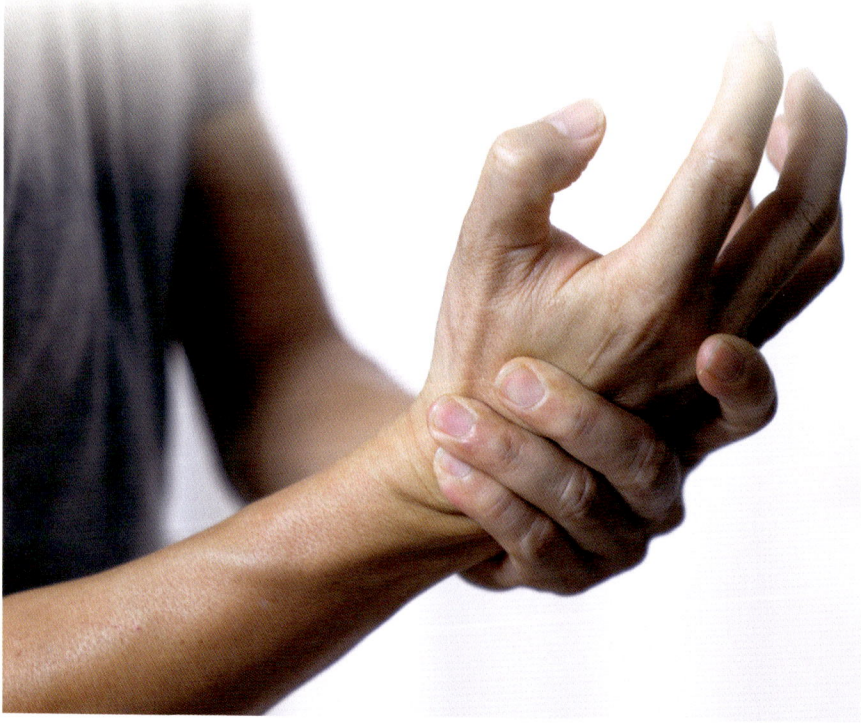

General Warning Signs

The following general symptoms indicate that something may be wrong with your body:

- aches and pains
- fever, especially over 101 degrees Fahrenheit
- coughing
- sneezing
- unexplainable weight gain or loss
- sores that don't heal
- a rash
- feeling strange or unusual
- dizziness
- problems sleeping
- feeling overly tired

Common Allergy Symptoms

- frequent runny nose

- itchy, watery eyes

- symptoms that occur during certain seasons

- symptoms that do not improve after taking antibiotics

Signs of a Bacterial Infection

- fever

- cough with rust- or green-colored mucus

- pain in a specific area

- symptoms that improve after taking antibiotics

What You Should Know About Allergies

Common Allergies

- pollen
- dust mites
- mold
- latex rubber
- animal dander
- certain foods
- bee and other insect stings

Possible Symptoms

- **Mild:** Rash or hives; itchy, watery eyes; mild congestion; affects one area of the body
- **Moderate:** Difficulty breathing; itching, hives, or swelling that spreads
- **Severe:** Can include swelling of the throat, extreme difficulty breathing, stomach pain, cramps, vomiting, diarrhea, hives, dizziness, and confusion. These symptoms can come on suddenly and be life-threatening.

Treatment

- Avoid the cause of the allergy.
- Take an oral medicine to stop the itching, swelling, and congestion.
- Use an oral or inhaled medicine to ease breathing difficulty.
- Get allergy shots, if needed.
- Use an EpiPen, if prescribed by a doctor.
- Call 911 or go to the emergency room at the first sign of a severe reaction, such as swelling of the throat and difficulty breathing.

Viral Versus Bacterial Infections

Do you know the difference between a viral and a bacterial infection? Viruses cause viral infections. Bacteria cause bacterial infections.

Often, the symptoms of the two conditions are the same. But the treatments are different.

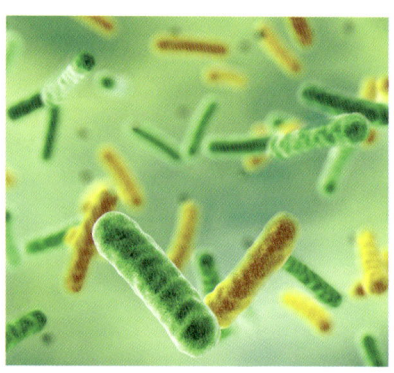

Type of Infection	Illnesses Caused	Treatment Needed
Viral	• Cold or runny nose • Most coughs and bronchitis (chest cold) • Most sore throats • Chicken pox • COVID-19 • Influenza • Hepatitis	• Rest • Drink fluids • Run a humidifier • Avoid smoke and pollution • Take a painkiller or decongestant • See a doctor to treat a serious condition
Bacterial	• Strep throat • Urinary tract infections • Skin infections • Tuberculosis	• Antibiotics—see a doctor
Can be either viral or bacterial	• Pneumonia • Ear infections • Sinus infections • Meningitis • Diarrhea	• See a doctor to find out what you have and how to treat it

Antibiotics: "Wonder Drugs"

Antibiotics are drugs that fight bacterial infections. The first antibiotic was penicillin. It was discovered in the late 1920s and became widely available for use in the 1940s. Penicillin was considered a "wonder drug" because of the number of lives it saved. Before the discovery of this drug, people often died from bacterial infections.

Today, antibiotics are some of the most frequently prescribed medicines. But taking them incorrectly can do you more harm than good.

Antibiotics work by killing off all the bacteria in your body. In most cases, you start to feel better almost immediately after starting to take an antibiotic.

But the effectiveness of antibiotics has two drawbacks:

1. **Antibiotics kill the good bacteria in your body along with the bad bacteria.** Good bacteria are needed to stay healthy.
2. **If you take antibiotics often, the bad bacteria in your body can begin to resist the drugs.** When this happens, antibiotics won't work to treat infection anymore. To avoid having this happen, don't take antibiotics unless you have a bacterial infection.

Chapter 2
First Aid and Emergency Care

Last summer, Kim took a first aid class through the American Red Cross. She learned how to treat common injuries, such as insect bites, small cuts, minor muscle strains, and bruises.

Kim also learned how to recognize an emergency and where to get help in emergency situations. Having this knowledge may help her save a life.

Medical Emergencies

You should call for help when you or someone you're with experiences any of the following:

- a large or deep wound or burn
- bleeding that won't stop
- continuous, nonstop vomiting or diarrhea
- a severe facial, head, neck, or back injury
- sudden, severe, or continuing pain, especially a headache
- choking
- a very high fever
- blacking out
- extreme behavior changes, such as confusion
- seizures
- extreme chest pain
- evidence of poisoning, even without physical symptoms

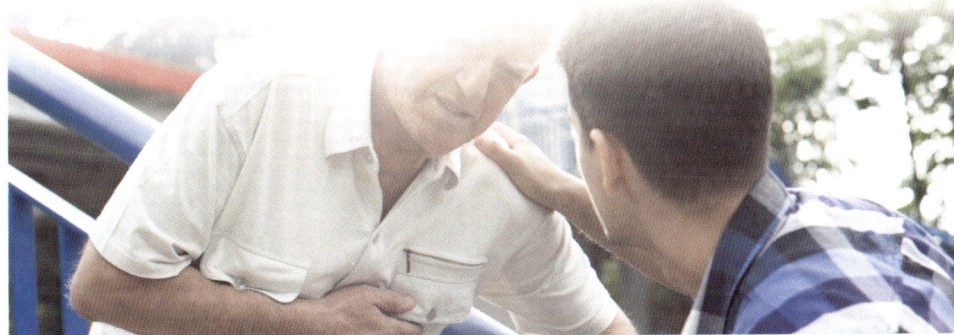

Dialing 911

If Kim sees someone with any of these signs, she calls to get help from emergency medical services (EMS). In the U.S., that number is 911.

When Kim calls, she knows to give her name and phone number. She also tells the EMS dispatcher the exact location where help is needed. This includes the address, apartment number, closest cross street, and nearby landmarks. Kim is also ready to answer all questions. Her training has taught her not to hang up the phone until she is told to. It has also made Kim aware of the need to follow all instructions.

The Facts About 911

- **The 911 system was set up in 1967.** The U.S. government wanted to create a single nationwide number to make emergency calls to police departments. The Federal Communications Commission worked with the nation's largest telephone company to set up the number.

- **The first 911 call in the United States was made in 1968.** Gradually, towns and cities across the country set up 911 service.

- **Making a 911 call from a landline telephone will probably get help more quickly than making a call from a cell phone.** Landline phones are tied to locations, but cell phones are not.

- **Calling 911 as a joke is against the law in most states.** But if you call 911 by mistake, don't hang up. Explain what happened so the dispatcher will know there's no emergency.

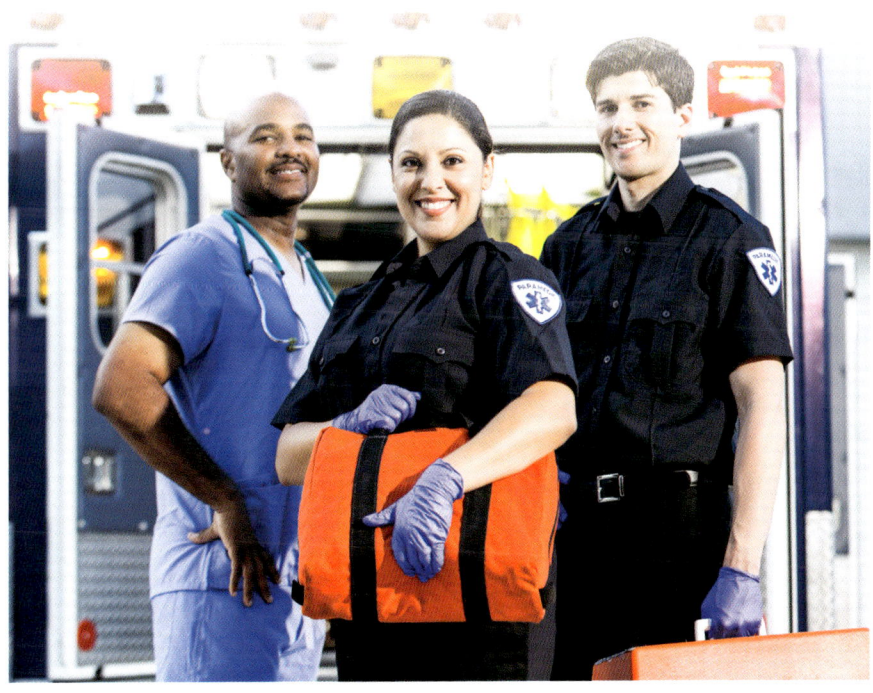

Going to the Clinic Versus the Emergency Room

Sometimes, a medical condition seems urgent but not immediately life-threatening. For example, a sprained ankle or cut that doesn't spurt blood calls for a visit to a clinic or doctor's office—not the emergency room (ER).

If it's after hours at the clinic or Kim's primary care physician isn't available, she goes to the hospital ER. Going to the ER isn't her first choice though.

A visit to the ER is the most expensive kind of medical care. Also, getting medical attention there can take a very long time. Emergencies are handled first. This means that patients not experiencing emergencies may have to wait several hours to be seen. People who can get care elsewhere, like a clinic or urgent care center, should go there first.

Chapter 3
Prescription and Over-the-Counter Medicines

When Eric had an ear infection, his doctor prescribed an antibiotic to fight it. The doctor filled out a prescription form and gave it to Eric to take to the pharmacy. Eric also had the option of having the doctor's office call in or send the prescription to the pharmacy online. He could then stop by the pharmacy later and pick up the medicine.

A prescription form contains the name of the drug being prescribed and the proper dosage. It also tells how many times the prescription can be refilled and in what time frame.

Never Share Prescription Medicines

When Eric walked into the pharmacy, he saw his friend Jasper. Eric explained that he'd been to the doctor and showed Jasper the prescription.

"I have some of that medicine at home," Jasper said. "You can have mine. Save your money."

"No," Eric answered. "That's okay. I'll get my own."

Eric had heard that it's not a good idea to share prescription drugs. Sharing medicines can lead to dangerous drug interactions, wrong dosages, and allergic reactions, among other things.

Talk to the Pharmacist

Eric's family always had their prescriptions filled at Fred's Friendly Pharmacy. They had known Fred for years and trusted his professional judgment. Pharmacists aren't doctors, but they know a great deal about different kinds of medicines.

"Hi, Eric," Fred said. "Let's see what you've got here today."

Fred looked at Eric's prescription form and asked, "Will you accept a generic brand of this drug?"

Fred explained that a less familiar brand of drug would be much cheaper than the most well-known brand. He assured Eric that the medicine was the same. Eric agreed to accept the generic version.

A few minutes later, Fred came back to the counter. Eric's prescription was ready. Since Eric had not used the drug before, Fred explained the dosage instructions. He also explained the side effects the drug could cause.

"If you become sleepy, dizzy, or have a dry mouth, call your doctor," Fred warned.

Questions to Ask About Medications

To know what to expect from a medicine, ask your doctor or pharmacist these questions:

- What does this medicine do?
- When and how should it be taken?
- What side effects are possible?
- Does the medicine react with other drugs, supplements, foods, or drinks?
- Should I avoid certain activities while taking this medicine?
- What happens if I forget to take this medicine?
- How will I know if the medicine is helping?

SAFER Medicine

When taking any kind of medicine, always think SAFER:

- **S:** Speak up.
- **A:** Ask questions.
- **F:** Find the facts.
- **E:** Evaluate your choices.
- **R:** Read the label for guidance.

Reading a Prescription Label

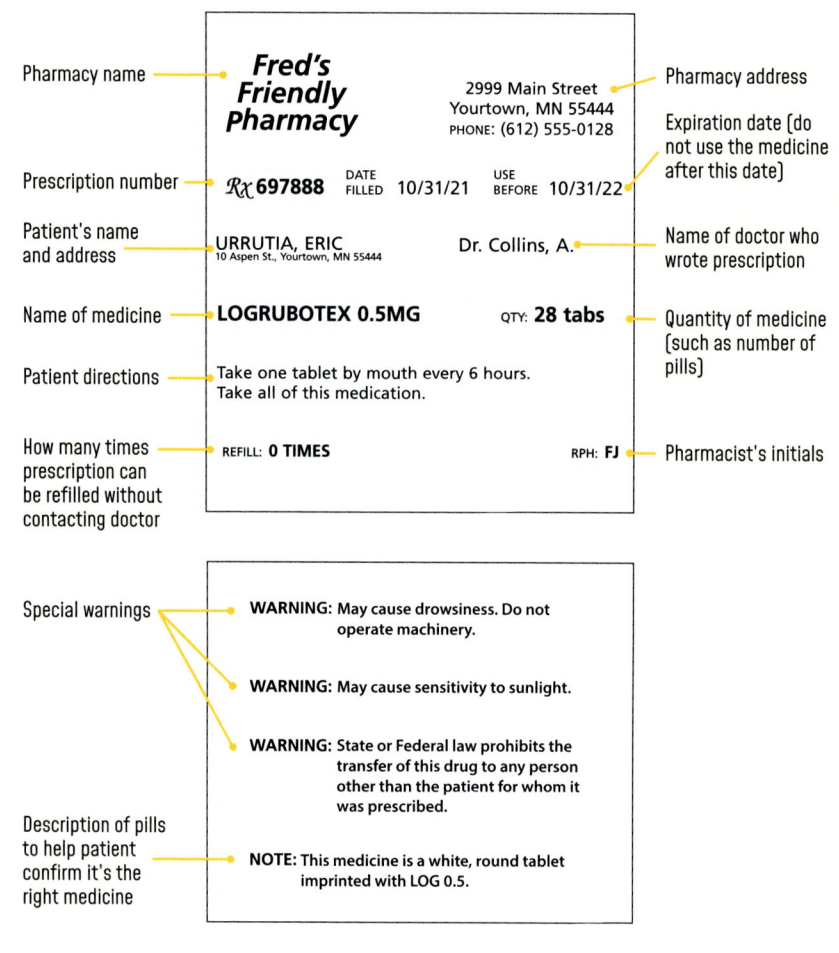

Over-the-Counter Medicines

You can find hundreds of over-the-counter (OTC) medicines on the shelves of your local supermarket or drugstore. Choosing one can be difficult. Whenever you have questions, talk to your doctor or pharmacist.

Common Over-the-Counter Medicines

The following chart lists some of the OTC products you may have at home in your medicine cabinet:

Type of Medication	Why It Is Used	Forms
Pain and fever medicine	To relieve pain and lower fever	Aspirin, acetaminophen, ibuprofen
Antacid	To treat indigestion, heartburn, and other stomach ailments	Chewable tablets, tablets that dissolve in water, liquids
Personal hygiene products	To clean the face and teeth	Soap or facial cleanser, toothpaste, dental floss, toothbrush, mouthwash
Sunscreens	To prevent sunburn	Lotions, creams, sprays

Guidelines for Buying, Storing, and Using Over-the-Counter Medicines

- **Always read a product's label.** If you don't know which product to buy, talk to your doctor or pharmacist.

- **Follow directions for OTC medicines carefully.** Avoid taking too little or too much. Don't assume that a drug is safe just because it doesn't require a prescription.

- **Many different brands are available of most OTC medicines.** An expensive name-brand product is not necessarily better than a less costly generic product. When in doubt, ask your doctor or pharmacist for advice.

- **All medicines can cause side effects, such as drowsiness.** Some may interact with foods or other medications. Read the label carefully so you know what to expect.

- **Pay attention to all warnings.** Not all medicines are safe for everyone. Conditions such as pregnancy or a heart ailment may make some OTC drugs dangerous.

- **Keep all medications out of children's reach.** No bottle is totally childproof.

Curing the Common Cold

Many people have a favorite cold remedy. But which remedies work, and which are bogus?

What Works

- drinking lots of clear fluids
- gargling with saltwater (mix ½ teaspoon per 1 cup of warm water)
- using saline nasal drops and sprays for congestion
- taking a zinc supplement
- using a humidifier
- eating chicken soup
- taking cough and cold medicines to ease symptoms
- using antihistamines

What Doesn't Work

- drinking alcohol or caffeine
- taking antibiotics
- for children under age 2, using cough and cold medicines

What Might Help

- taking vitamin C (especially before you get a cold)
- taking echinacea

Can You Use Expired Medicines?

Every medicine, whether prescription or over-the-counter, has an expiration date stamped on it. The medicine is supposed to be 100% effective until that date. Marking medicines with expiration dates became a U.S. law in 1979.

However, many medicines are still completely effective long past the expiration date. A study by the U.S. Food and Drug Administration (FDA) found that 90% of drugs were perfectly good 15 years after the expiration date.

Medical professionals agree that taking an expired medicine won't hurt you. But they warn that an old medicine may not be as effective as it's supposed to be. Liquid medicines may lose their effectiveness sooner than dry ones. If a liquid becomes cloudy or changes color, throw it away.

A few drugs should never be used past their expiration dates. These include nitroglycerin, insulin, epinephrine, and liquid antibiotics. They cannot be counted on to work.

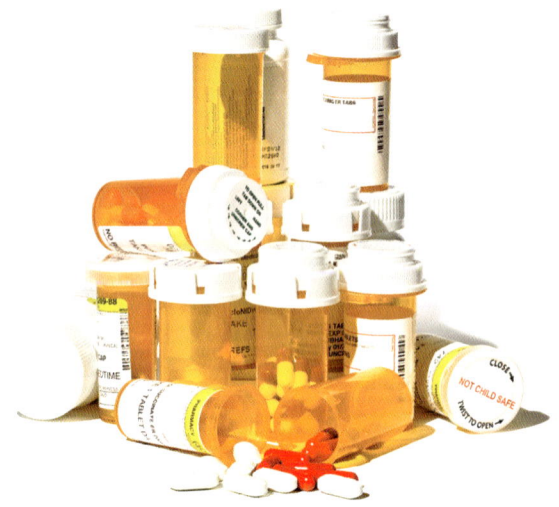

Chapter 4
Mental Health

Everyone faces mental stress and strain. We all feel sad or confused from time to time too. How do you deal with your emotions when life gets tough? What helps you relax? Where do you go for help?

Help Yourself

Take a deep breath. People in a hurry or under stress tend to take shallow breaths. When you feel tense, breathe deeply. Fill your lungs, count to four, and then let out the breath.

Meditation can also be helpful. This is the practice of spending time in quiet thought in order to relax. Many people focus on their breathing while meditating. The process helps them feel calmer and less distracted.

Another way to improve mental health is to improve your physical health. Keep active and fit. Exercise can melt away stress. At the end of a stressful day, go for a walk or shoot some hoops. Also eat well and get plenty of rest. Being well rested can make you feel more able to face life's challenges.

Doing creative activities can relax your mind and lift your spirit too. Try dancing, singing, painting, or drawing for enjoyment and relaxation.

Finally, some people like to reach for a "security blanket." Special items can make us feel safe when facing stress and tension. Wearing "lucky" sneakers might calm an athlete's nerves. Carrying a special coin might settle an actor's stage fright. What makes you feel safe and secure?

Confide in Others

Talk about what's bothering you. Just putting a problem into words can make you feel less anxious about it. Consider talking to your parents, trusted teachers, relatives, or friends. If you want what you say to stay private, let them know. Similarly, if someone confides in you about a problem, it is important to keep the information they tell you confidential, unless they are talking about harming themselves or others.

There are several different ways to open up about your troubles:

- **When stress gets really hard to handle, go to someone you trust.** It might be a parent, a favorite teacher, or an older brother or sister. You might want this person just to listen, or you might want his or her advice and support.

- **If you're uncomfortable talking to someone about your problems, try writing about them in a journal.** Organizing your thoughts in writing might help you sort them out and see situations more clearly.

CHAPTER 4: MENTAL HEALTH | 89

Seek Professional Help

At times, you might need to share your feelings with a professional. A mental health counselor or therapist is trained to help people sort through their problems.

At a therapy session, a professional may meet with you one-on-one, with you and family, or with you and a group of people. You'll learn about your strengths and weaknesses and discuss positive coping skills. In a support group, you'll get a chance to express your emotions with others who are in a similar situation. Therapy can also give you tools to help make changes in your life and communicate your feelings more clearly.

Types of Therapists and Counselors

Professional therapists and counselors have a variety of training and backgrounds, including some type of graduate-level degree. They may be psychologists, social workers, marriage and family therapists, or psychiatrists.

All of these professionals are qualified to provide counseling services. But in most states, only psychiatrists are allowed to prescribe medicines. That's because psychiatrists are trained as medical doctors. If you need medicine and are not seeing a psychiatrist, your counselor will make a referral to a psychiatrist or your regular doctor for a prescription.

How can you find a good therapist or counselor? Ask people you trust to recommend someone. You might ask family members, a close friend, or your family doctor. At school, you can find help by talking to a trusted teacher or guidance counselor.

Keep in mind that the first therapist you see might not be right for you. If that happens, keep looking. Counselors and therapists have different personalities and styles. To get the best support and guidance, you'll need to find someone who's a good fit for you.

Tips for Finding a Therapist or Counselor

Before you make an appointment, interview several therapists or counselors over the phone. Ask these questions:

- What are your professional qualifications, including education, license, or certification?
- What area do you specialize in?
- How long have you been practicing?
- What are your fees? How are they billed?
- Do you accept my insurance? Are reduced fees or payment plans available?

At your first appointment, ask these questions to help determine if this is the right therapist or counselor for you:

- How can you help me with my problems?
- What kind of treatment do you use?
- How long will counseling last?

SECTION 4

Dealing With Stress

We usually think of stress negatively. People talk of feeling "stressed out." This can be from pressures at work or school. It can come from parents and relationships as well. But stress isn't always bad. It can be good for us. Stress can push us to try new things, finish projects, and better ourselves. Good stress is called "eustress." Bad stress is called "distress." When left unmanaged, distress can negatively affect our lives and our bodies.

A Stressful Situation

Tim's parents divorced. He and his mom moved to a new town. His first day of school did not go well. Three of his classes were in the middle of units of study and had big tests coming up. One class had already assigned group projects. Now Tim had a ton of homework to do in order to catch up.

After school, his car didn't start. This made him late for his new job at a local coffee shop. His boss yelled at him. Then Tim messed up several customers' orders.

Back at home, Tim couldn't focus on his homework. His head hurt, and he snapped at his mom when she asked if he was okay. That night, he had trouble getting to sleep.

The next morning, he woke up with a cold. His mom told him not to go to school or work. Tim felt worried that he would fall further behind at school and his boss would be mad at him for missing work.

Chapter 1
The Effects of Stress on the Body

Stress is a natural reaction to life experiences. When we experience stress, the body releases **hormones** in response. We can feel this in various parts of our body, from a racing heart to rapid breathing. These hormones prepare the body to respond to whatever is causing the stress.

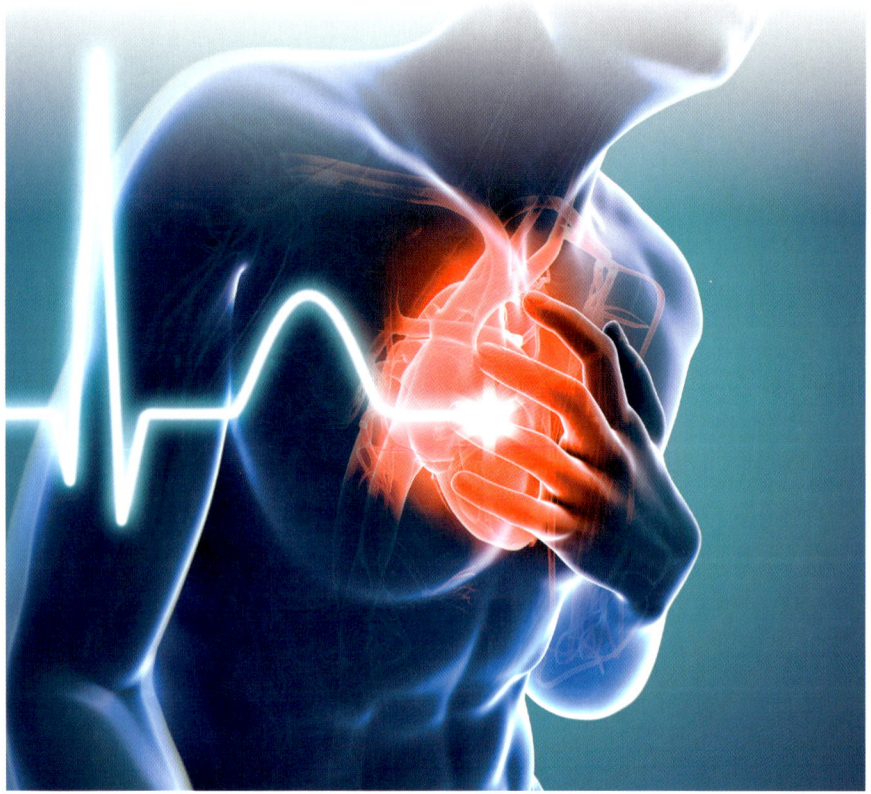

Stress responses should only last for a short time. Once you deal with the stressor, they should go away. However, when stress levels stay elevated, your health can suffer. Chronic stress can cause a variety of symptoms, including:

- irritable moods
- anxiety
- depression
- headaches
- insomnia
- weight loss or weight gain

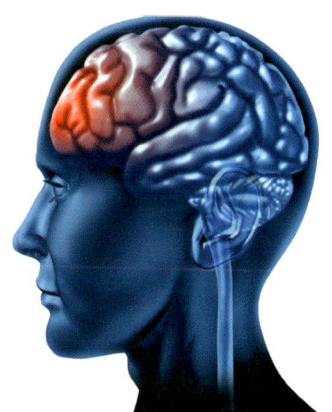

Effects of Stress on Mood and Behavior

On Mood	On Behavior
Anxiety	Overeating or undereating
Restlessness	Angry outbursts
Lack of motivation or focus	Abusing drugs or alcohol
Feeling overwhelmed	Tobacco use
Irritability or anger	Social withdrawal
Sadness or depression	Exercising less often

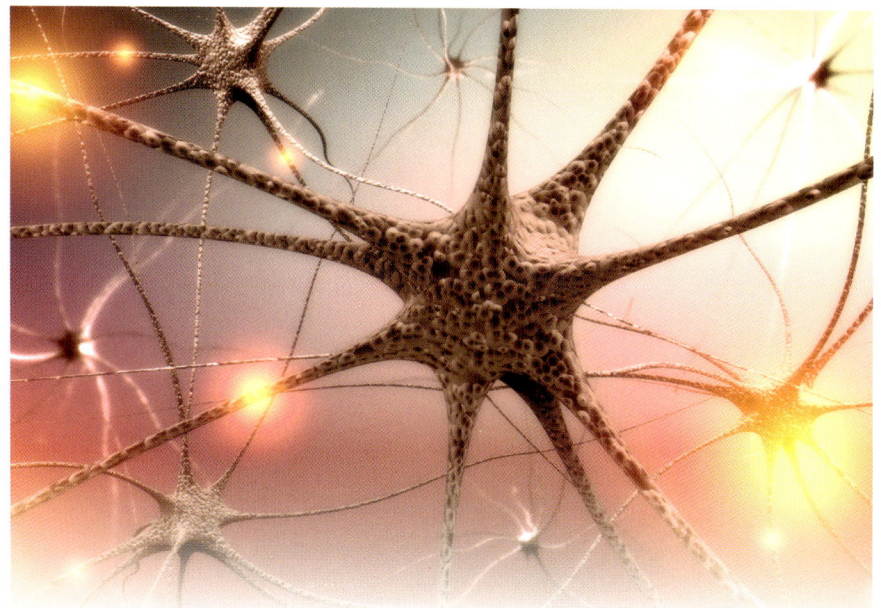

Central Nervous System

When stressed, the central nervous system releases a "fight or flight" response. This makes the heart beat faster and sends blood rushing to your muscles, heart, and other important organs. It is preparing your body to either deal with or run away from the stressor.

With chronic stress, this response stays active. When a person remains in fight-or-flight mode, it can lead to anxiety, high blood pressure, depression, and addiction.

Cardiovascular System

When you are under stress, your heart pumps faster. Your body also rushes blood to your muscles. This raises your blood pressure. Frequent stress will make the heart work too hard. Raised blood pressure puts you at risk for a stroke or heart attack.

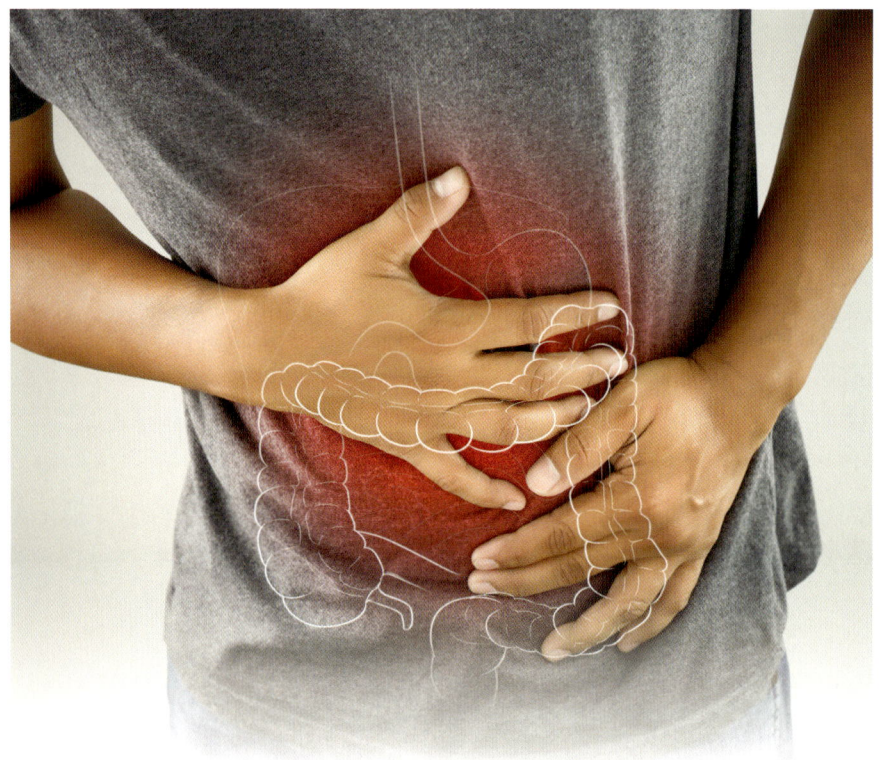

Digestive System

Stress causes the body to release extra glucose. This gives you a boost of energy. Chronic stress causes glucose to keep getting pumped into the body. It can lead to the development of diabetes. People experiencing chronic stress are also more likely to have heartburn, acid reflux, and stomach ulcers.

Immune System

As time passes, stress weakens your immune system. People under chronic stress are more likely to get sick from the common cold or flu. They are also more susceptible to infections. Stress can increase the time it takes for your body to heal too.

Chapter 2
Recognizing Stressors

Dealing with stress begins with being able to recognize what is causing the stress. There are many common stressors in our daily lives. A deadline for a tough school project may be coming up. Your boss might be unhappy with your work performance. You or a loved one may be struggling with an illness. Perhaps your family is having financial problems.

All of these things can cause stress. It is important to take steps to recognize and ease these stressors before they lead to health problems.

Know Your Stressors

Stress can come from internal and external sources. Make a list of people, situations, or thoughts that trigger you to feel stressed. This can help you identify your stressors.

External stressors might include:

- major life changes, such as moving, divorce, or a death in the family
- loud noises and distractions in your environment
- meeting new people
- unpredictable events, such as a house fire or getting laid off from your job
- work stress
- relationship problems

Internal stressors might include:

- your fears
- a feeling of not being in control of a situation
- your thoughts and attitudes about yourself or others
- unmet expectations

Starting a Stress Journal

A stress journal can help you pinpoint the common stressors in your life. Each time you feel stressed, write about it in your journal. Keeping a daily log will enable you to see patterns and common themes. Include:

- what caused your stress
- how you felt, both physically and emotionally
- how you acted in response
- what you did to make yourself feel better

Chapter 3
Finding Ways to Cope

Once you know more about what is stressing you out, it's time to learn how to cope with those stressors. The following steps can help.

Step 1: Practice the 4 As

Stress often comes at predictable times. It may come during a certain class at school, on the job, or at family gatherings. When you know stress is coming, you can either change the situation or your reaction to it using the 4 *As*.

- **Avoid unnecessary stress.** Limit the time you spend around people who stress you out. Learn to say no to situations that cause stress. Remove stressful things from your to-do list.

- **Alter the situation.** When you can't avoid a stressful situation, try altering it. Talk out your feelings instead of keeping them inside. Be willing to compromise.

- **Adapt to the stressor.** If a situation can't be avoided or altered, try adapting to it. Is it possible to view the stressor from a positive perspective? Can you find the good in it?

- **Accept the things you can't change.** Some stress is unavoidable. A serious illness, the death of a loved one, or getting laid off can't be prevented. In these cases, accepting, rather than fighting, the stress is the best option. Talk to friends or loved ones you trust about your situation. Look for the upside. Make a plan for the future.

Step 2: Exercise

Physical activity is a huge stress reliever. Exercise releases endorphins that make you feel good. Try working out for 30 minutes or more each day. Go for a walk. Take the stairs instead of the elevator at work. Dance around your living room to some music. Play basketball with a friend. Pay attention to how your body feels as you exercise. Do you feel yourself relaxing? Are your thoughts clearer?

Step 3: Connect With Others

Spending time with people we love can have a calming effect. Reach out to friends and family. Get together for a game night, or just have a nice chat on the phone. Talk to them about your problems if you want to. You might also just focus on having a fun time together. Taking your mind off of stress for a while can help you recharge.

Step 4: Learn to Relieve Stress

Moments of stress will pop up throughout your day. It is important to be able to relieve stress in the moment so that it doesn't build up. The easiest way to reduce stress is to take a few deep breaths. Focus on a happy image or thought. This can be a special photo or the lyrics to your favorite song. These small things can help you refocus and stay calm.

Chapter 4
Post-Traumatic Stress Disorder

Post-traumatic stress disorder (PTSD) is a condition that can affect anyone who has seen or experienced something horrible and frightening. This may have been a terrorist act, a serious car accident, or an assault. Often, soldiers who see violence in war are affected by PTSD. But anyone who has experienced trauma may develop PTSD.

Symptoms of PTSD include:

- recurring, unwanted memories of the event
- avoidance of thinking or talking about the event
- avoidance of places or people that remind you of the event
- negative changes in your thoughts or mood
- changes in your physical and emotional reactions (being jumpy and always on guard, having trouble sleeping, irritability, self-destructive behavior)

Flashbacks

PTSD can vary in intensity. A person with PTSD may experience more symptoms when feeling stressed in general. Many people with PTSD struggle with flashbacks. These are moments when people feel as though they are reliving their trauma. A flashback is temporary. People experiencing them may stay aware of their present surroundings, or they may lose all awareness. For example, a soldier returns home from war. His family is excited to spend time with him. They decide to go to the local fair. That night, the fair closes down with a fireworks display. The loud explosions and flashing lights upset the soldier. Suddenly, he feels as though he is back in a war zone.

When to Seek Help

If you are having any of the symptoms of PTSD, see a doctor or mental health professional as soon as possible. Getting treatment can help prevent PTSD symptoms from getting worse.

Sometimes people with PTSD are so overwhelmed by their thoughts and memories that they consider suicide. If you have thoughts like this, get help right away. Reach out to a trusted friend or loved one, call a suicide hotline, or see your doctor. Treatment can improve your PTSD.

Triggers

PTSD flashbacks are often set off by triggers. These are reminders of the traumatic event. When a person experiences a trigger, they may suddenly become very afraid. They may also experience memories of their trauma. A trigger can be anything that the person associates with the traumatic event. Examples of triggers include:

- smells
- sounds
- hearing or reading certain words or stories
- movies or news reports about similar events
- feelings and sensations, such as pain, that remind you of the event
- encounters with people involved in or related to the event
- visits to the place where the event happened
- situations that make you feel out of control
- anniversaries tied to the event

If you feel as if you are in danger, that is a sign you have experienced a PTSD trigger. It is important to learn your triggers so you can better avoid them. A mental health care professional can help you identify triggers and find coping strategies.

A Happy, Healthy Life

Health and wellness are important aspects of life. However, maintaining good health includes much more than just eating right and exercising. Good health and wellness require a holistic approach that includes the mind, body, and spirit. Make the time to care for your whole self, and reap the rewards of a healthy lifestyle.

Glossary

aerobic exercise: movement that works the heart and lungs to make them stronger

ailment: an illness

anesthetic: a drug that numbs all or part of the body

antibiotic: a medicine made to kill harmful bacteria

artery: a large blood vessel that moves blood away from the heart

bacteria: tiny forms of life that can make a person sick; germs

balance: the state of having your weight evenly distributed so that you are able to stay upright

central nervous system: the brain and spinal cord

contagious: able to be passed from person to person

contract: to come down with an illness

coverage: financial assistance provided by an insurance policy

dependent: supported by someone or something else

dermatologist: a doctor who specializes in caring for the skin

diagnosis: the identification of an illness or disease

dosage: the amount of a drug that a patient should take at a certain time

endorphins: chemicals in the body that produce feelings of well-being

extract: to remove something by pulling or cutting it out

fluoride: a chemical added to toothpaste that keeps teeth healthy

generic: not sold under a brand name

gland: a part of the body that makes a substance that the body uses

glucose: a source of energy in a person's body; also known as blood sugar

health insurance: financial coverage provided by a company for medical expenses

hormone: a substance in the body that affects growth and development

hygiene: the things people do to keep themselves and the areas around them clean so that they have good health

impacted: growing under another tooth

infectious: able to pass on germs or a disease

mineral: a chemical important to health, like iron

nutrient: a substance needed for life and growth

policy: a document from an insurance company that outlines coverage amounts and rules and restrictions related to receiving benefits

premium: the amount that must be paid to keep insurance in effect for a given amount of time

referral: the act of sending a patient to another place for treatment

severe: very bad

side effect: something that happens in response to a drug or chemical in addition to what was supposed to happen; often unpleasant

specialist: someone with specific knowledge and skill in a particular area

sterilization: the process of making something clean and germ-free

susceptible: likely to be affected or infected

symptom: a change in the body or mind that shows something is wrong

treatment: the course of action a medical professional prescribes to deal with an illness or heal an injury

virus: a very small molecule that takes over a cell in order to reproduce, often causing illness

vitamin: a substance in food that humans and animals must eat to stay healthy

LIFE SKILLS HANDBOOKS

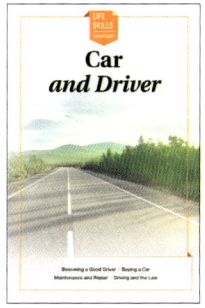

9781680219821

9781680219913

9781680219838

9781680219845

9781680219852

9781680219869

9781680219883

9781680219890

9781680219906

9781680219876

For more information, visit:
www.sdlback.com/life-skills-handbooks